CATERING WORKSHOP

Feeding a Hungry Crowd

Megan Borgert-Spaniol

An imprint of Abdo Publishing
abdobooks.com

ABDOBOOKS.COM

Published by Abdo Publishing, a division of ABDO, PO Box 398166, Minneapolis, Minnesota 55439. Copyright © 2024 by Abdo Consulting Group, Inc. International copyrights reserved in all countries. No part of this book may be reproduced in any form without written permission from the publisher. Abdo & Daughters™ is a trademark and logo of Abdo Publishing.

Printed in the United States of America, North Mankato, Minnesota
052023
092023

Design: Aruna Rangarajan and Emily O'Malley, Mighty Media, Inc.
Production: Mighty Media, Inc.
Editor: Ruthie Van Oosbree
Cover Photographs: Mighty Media, Inc.; Shutterstock Images
Recipes: Megan Borgert-Spaniol
Interior Photographs: Henry Bryan Hall/Wikimedia Commons, p. 6 (top left); iStockphoto, pp. 5 (bottom), 13 (bottom right, middle right), 15 (middle left, bottom right), 17 (top right), 24, 26, 56, 60, 61 (bottom); Mighty Media, Inc., pp. 30 (cups), 32 (all), 33 (all), 34–35, 36 (chicken Parmesan), 38 (all), 39 (all), 40–41, 42 (potato salad), 44 (all), 45 (all), 46–47, 48 (brownies), 50 (all), 51 (all), 52–53; Ministry of Information Photo Division Photographer/Wikimedia Commons, p. 6 (top right); Robin van Rossum/Wikimedia Commons, p. 8 (left); Shutterstock Images, pp. 3, 4, 5 (top), 6 (bottom), 8 (right), 9, 10, 11 (all), 12 (all), 13 (top right, left all), 14, 15 (top, bottom left, middle right), 16 (all), 17 (top left, bottom left, bottom right), 18 (all), 19 (all), 20 (all), 21 (all), 22, 23 (all), 25 (all), 27 (all), 28, 29 (all), 30 (background), 36 (background), 42 (background), 48 (background), 54 (all), 55 (all), 57, 58 (all), 59 (all), 61 (top)
Design Elements: Shutterstock Images

The following manufacturers/names appearing in this book are trademarks: GoodCook®, Wilton®

Library of Congress Control Number: 2022948838

PUBLISHER'S CATALOGING-IN-PUBLICATION DATA

Names: Borgert-Spaniol, Megan, author.
Title: Catering workshop: feeding a hungry crowd / by Megan Borgert-Spaniol
Other title: feeding a hungry crowd
Description: Minneapolis, Minnesota : Abdo Publishing, 2024 | Series: Kitchen to career | Includes online resources and index.
Identifiers: ISBN 9781098291389 (lib. bdg.) | ISBN 9781098277840 (ebook)
Subjects: LCSH: Food--Juvenile literature. | Cooking--Juvenile literature. | Caterers and catering--Juvenile literature. | Quantity cooking--Juvenile literature. | Food service--Juvenile literature. | Cooking for large numbers--Juvenile literature. | Occupations--Juvenile literature.
Classification: DDC 641.3--dc23

CONTENTS

Making a Career in the Kitchen 5

The Basics 7

Getting Started 11

◆ **Spinach & Feta Cups 31**

◆ **Chicken Parmesan 37**

◆ **Potato Salad...................... 43**

◆ **Brownie Bites 49**

Presentation & Beyond 54

Careers in the Kitchen 57

Glossary 62

Online Resources 63

Index 64

MAKING A CAREER IN THE KITCHEN

Do you enjoy the challenge of preparing food for large groups? Do you love to dream up fun ways to serve and present your dishes? Can you see yourself creating menus that are tailored to specific events? If your answer to these questions is yes, you might be suited to a career in catering.

Becoming a catering professional takes training and hard work. It takes dedication to service, quality, and safety. But if you have a passion for catering, you may find that the dedication comes naturally and the hard work is worthwhile.

In this book, you'll learn about the history of catering and how it is influenced by current events and popular culture. You'll become familiar with basic ingredients, tools, and techniques used to feed a hungry crowd. You'll practice using these ingredients, tools, and techniques in a few basic recipes. Then, you'll try following your own tastes and inspirations to modify recipes. Finally, you'll learn how you might turn your passion for cooking into a career.

The earliest recorded catering event in the United States was a ball to celebrate British general William Howe (*pictured*) in 1778.

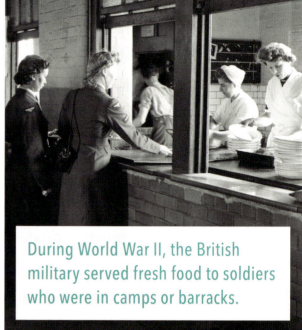

During World War II, the British military served fresh food to soldiers who were in camps or barracks.

Most event venues have a full kitchen on-site and offer either buffet or plated catering services.

THE BASICS

CATERING ACROSS THE AGES

Catering is the service of providing food and sometimes drinks for large gatherings of people. This practice dates back thousands of years to feasts and banquets in China and Egypt. Later, ancient Greeks and Romans offered catering services at inns. Through the Middle Ages, it was primarily members of the royal and noble classes who used catering services for extravagant meals.

In the United States, the earliest recorded catered event took place in Philadelphia in 1778. The event was a ball to celebrate the departure of a British general. But it wasn't until after World War II that the catering industry really boomed. Companies that had provided food services for the war effort turned their attention to catering. Meanwhile, the growing economy created greater demand for catering services as more people and businesses had the means to host large gatherings.

Over the decades, the catering industry grew larger and more competitive. As more catering companies were established, many hotels and restaurants also joined the market by adding in-house catering departments. Caterers set themselves apart with floral arrangements, linens, tableware, and other stylistic touches they provided with their food services.

The modern catering industry can be divided into four types of services. Wedding caterers make and serve food for guests at wedding receptions. The catering staff serve plated meals to guests at their tables, or they set up a buffet where guests serve themselves. Corporate caterers provide meals for company functions, from holiday parties to regional conferences. In addition to plated meals and buffets, corporate caterers also provide boxed meals for less formal gatherings, such as workday meetings.

Concession catering is another type of catering service. It refers to the food provided at major sporting events, competitions, and concerts. Concession caterers focus on providing a limited menu of popular foods that can be produced in large quantities for speedy service. Finally, social event

> In Europe, many trains have a catering service where commuters can purchase drinks, snacks, and sometimes small meals.

> Every catering company is different. Some provide just the food and service. Others may offer everything needed for an event, from plates to decorations to tents, in addition to the food.

catering provides food for smaller events, such as birthday parties, baby showers, and other more personal gatherings. For these events, caterers provide everything from snacks and appetizers to buffets and boxed or plated meals.

No matter the venue or event, catering trends may be influenced by current events. For example, the COVID-19 pandemic forced caterers to adapt to new safety standards. Instead of setting out large platters of appetizers, caterers portioned out small bites into individual containers. This kept guests from congregating for too long at serving tables. It also reduced the risk of germs spreading via serving utensils.

Popular culture also influences catering trends. In an age when people share pictures of food on social media, caterers have gotten more creative with their presentations. Donut walls, colorful macaron displays, and mason jar salads provide guests with tasty bites and social media-worthy photos.

What menu items would you offer if you catered an event? How would you present and serve them? In the following pages, you'll learn about common ingredients, tools, and techniques in preparing tasty foods for large crowds. Soon you'll be ready to feed your own gathering of hungry guests!

Some catering companies follow trends to create fun, photo-worthy experiences for guests, such as donut walls.

GETTING STARTED

INGREDIENTS

Get familiar with some of the ingredients you'll see in this book's recipes

CANDY MELTS

Candy melts are sugar-based flavored disks that melt into a smooth coating for desserts. They come in a variety of colors and are typically vanilla flavored. Candy melts can be used for dipping desserts like brownie pops, poured into molds, piped from a pastry bag, and more.

CHEESE

Cheese comes in hundreds of varieties that range from soft and creamy to firm and salty. Ricotta is a soft, fluffy cheese with a lightly sweet-salty flavor. Feta is a crumbly, salty cheese. Brie is a soft, creamy cheese encased in an edible rind of white mold.

Mozzarella is a semi-soft cheese with a creamy flavor. Parmesan is a hard, salty cheese that's often grated over finished dishes.

CHICKEN BREASTS

Chicken breast is a cut of lean meat from the front of a chicken. Chicken cutlets are breasts cut in half horizontally. Cutlets have a more uniform thickness than breasts and therefore cook more evenly.

COCOA POWDER

Cocoa powder is the dried, ground solids that come from cacao beans. This ingredient is unsweetened, making it slightly bitter on its own. But when combined with a sweetener like sugar, cocoa powder brings a deep chocolate flavor to desserts and drinks.

CONDIMENTS

Condiments are sauces or liquids that add flavor to food. Mayonnaise is a creamy and slightly tangy condiment made of oil, eggs, and vinegar or lemon juice. Mustard, made of whole or ground mustard seeds, is also made tangy with vinegar. Some recipes call for sour flavors from highly acidic condiments such as apple cider vinegar and lemon juice.

CORNSTARCH

Cornstarch is a fine powder made from corn. It is used as a thickening agent for sauces and soups. It is also often mixed with flour to make breading for fried food. The cornstarch helps make the breading extra crispy when fried.

DAIRY

Heavy cream, also called heavy whipping cream, is the thick part of fresh milk that rises to the top due to its high fat content. This ingredient adds creaminess to many dishes. Butter is a fat typically made from cow's milk. It lends creaminess and rich flavor to dishes. In baked goods, butter adds moistness and tenderness to the texture.

EGGS

Eggs help bind batters for baked goods. They also act as leaveners because their proteins trap air bubbles. In fried foods, eggs help the breading stick to the food.

FLOUR

The recipes in this book call for all-purpose flour. This is a blend of wheat flours that can be used to make a variety of baked goods. Flour is also used in breading foods for frying. It forms the first layer of the breading, which helps seal in moisture and gives the egg wash something to adhere to.

HERBS

Parsley is a leafy herb with a clean, lightly bitter flavor. It is often sprinkled as a garnish on top of finished dishes for added flavor and color. Chives are grasslike herbs that taste of mild onion and garlic. They can be added to a variety of dishes.

KOSHER SALT & BLACK PEPPER

Salt is a mineral that brings its own flavor while also enhancing other flavors. The recipes in this book call for kosher salt, which is made of coarser grains than table salt. Black pepper comes from berries called peppercorns that are dried and ground up. It adds depth and spice to all kinds of dishes.

MARINARA SAUCE

Marinara sauce is a tomato sauce flavored with aromatics such as onions, garlic, and herbs.

OIL

Oils are liquid fats used in cooking and baking.
Vegetable oil has a neutral flavor and can withstand high heat. This makes it a go-to oil for frying foods, which requires high temperatures. It is also used to grease pans.

PANKO

Panko is a Japanese style of breadcrumbs made from crustless white bread. The bread is dried, ground into flakes, and then toasted. Panko is used as a breading for meats and vegetables. Its texture results in a light and crunchy coating.

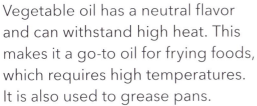

PHYLLO SHELLS

Phyllo is a delicate pastry made of layers of paper-thin dough. Making phyllo from scratch is a tedious process. Most cooks and bakers purchase premade phyllo that has been mass-produced with the help of machines. Store-bought phyllo comes in sheets that can be shaped by the baker. It also comes in pre-baked shells that can be filled.

SPICES

Spices add strong flavors to dishes. Garlic powder and onion powder are dehydrated and ground-up versions of the spicy-sweet ingredients they are named after. Garlic salt is mix of salt and garlic powder.

VANILLA EXTRACT

Pure vanilla extract is made by soaking vanilla beans in an alcohol solution. This pulls out the flavors of the vanilla beans and concentrates them in liquid form. In baked goods, vanilla extract helps enhance other flavors, such as chocolate.

KITCHEN TOOLS

Get familiar with some of the supplies you'll see in this book's recipes

BAKING SHEET

A baking sheet is a pan with a shallow rim around all four sides or no rim at all.

BROILER

The broiler is the part of an oven that exposes dishes to high heat for quick browning. It is usually located on the ceiling of the oven, but in some ovens the broiler is in a drawer at the bottom of the appliance.

COLANDER

A colander is a bowl with drainage holes used to separate cooking water from the cooked food, such as pasta or potatoes. Colanders are also helpful tools for holding fresh produce while rinsing it.

COOLING RACK

A cooling rack allows air to circulate around hot food, helping it cool faster than it would on a solid surface.

DUTCH OVEN

A Dutch oven is a heavy, durable pot used to cook food on the stove or in the oven. Most Dutch ovens are made of cast iron, allowing them to withstand high temperatures and retain heat. They can be used to fry chicken, slow-cook beef, and even bake bread!

ELECTRIC MIXER

Both stand mixers and handheld mixers use electricity to whip ingredients, such as cooked potatoes. It is possible to whip mashed potatoes without an electric mixer—it just takes a little more time and muscle!

LOLLIPOP STICKS

Lollipop sticks are sticks about 3 to 6 inches (7.6 to 15.2 cm) long made of tightly rolled paper. Bakers use these sticks to make cake pops, brownie pops, and other treats on sticks. If you don't have lollipop sticks, try using paper straws, skewers, or craft sticks instead.

MINI MUFFIN PAN

A muffin pan is a baking pan with indented cups that hold batter for baking. Mini muffin pans have cups that are about one-third the size of those in regular muffin pans. They are used to make bite-size desserts, such as mini brownies, cupcakes, or tarts.

PARCHMENT PAPER

Parchment paper is a heat-resistant nonstick paper that helps prevent ingredients, such as batters, from sticking to baking pans. When making brownies or other desserts that bake in deep pans, cut the parchment longer than the length of the pan. This creates flaps of parchment that aid in lifting the baked dessert from the pan.

SAUCEPAN

A saucepan is a piece of cookware with a flat circular base; tall, straight sides; and one long handle. It is meant for cooking liquids on the stove. In this book, a saucepan is used to heat up heavy cream and butter on the stove for mashed potatoes.

SIEVE

A sieve, or sifter, is a bowl-shaped utensil with a long handle. The bowl is made of wire mesh that breaks up lumps in dry ingredients. Bakers use this tool to cover foods with a fine dusting of powdered sugar.

THERMOMETERS

A meat thermometer measures the internal temperature of meat and fish. For an accurate reading, insert the thermometer into the thickest part of the meat. While meat thermometers read up to about 200°F, candy thermometers and deep-fry thermometers read up to about 400°F. Candy and deep-fry thermometers can both be used to measure oil temperature.

TONGS

Tongs are a kitchen tool made of two long metal arms joined at one end. Tongs are held in one hand and used to flip, transfer, or otherwise handle hot foods.

WHISK

A whisk is used to blend ingredients quickly and thoroughly. This includes dry ingredients, such as flour mixtures, and wet ingredients, such as eggs, dressings, and melted chocolate.

TERMS & TECHNIQUES

Get familiar with some of the terms and techniques you'll see in this book's recipes.

CHOPPING, DICING & MINCING

Chopping is a cutting technique that results in rough, uneven chunks of an ingredient.

Dicing is a more precise cutting technique that results in slightly smaller pieces of uniform size.

Mincing is cutting an ingredient into tiny pieces so its flavor spreads throughout a dish while its texture goes unnoticed.

DREDGING

To dredge is to coat a wet or moist ingredient with a dry ingredient before cooking. In this book, chicken is dredged in flour, dipped in egg, then coated with breadcrumbs before being fried in oil. Dredging is commonly used with meat and fish, but the technique also works for vegetables such as eggplant.

FORK-TENDER

Some recipes instruct you to cook a food until it is fork-tender. This means it should be tender enough to be easily pierced or cut with a fork. When making potato salad, be careful not to overcook the potatoes, or your salad will have the consistency of mashed potatoes.

GREASING THE PAN

Greasing a pan means covering it with a layer of fat before pouring batter or placing dough into the pan. The fat keeps the baked product from sticking to the pan. Unless a recipe calls for a specific fat, you can grease your pans with butter or any neutral oil, such as vegetable or canola oil. You can also use baking sprays, which contain oils mixed with flour.

MEASURING FLOUR

While pro bakers usually measure flour by weight, most recipes for home bakers include flour measurements by volume, or cups. To properly measure flour by volume, use a whisk to fluff the flour in the bag so it isn't packed. Then spoon the flour into your measuring cup. Run the straight edge of a table knife over the top of the cup to get rid of excess flour.

GARNISHING

Garnishes are ingredients used to embellish a finished dish with added color, texture, or flavor. Herbs are popular garnishes for savory dishes, as are nuts, seeds, and cheese. Desserts can be garnished with fruit sauce, chocolate shavings, citrus zest, powdered sugar, and more.

PREHEATING THE OVEN

Brownies and other baked goods rely on an initial blast of heat to kick-start their rise. That's why it's important to preheat your oven, or let it fully heat to the specified temperature, before you start baking.

SEASONING WITH SALT & PEPPER

Without salt and pepper, most dishes would taste bland. But too much salt and pepper will overpower the other flavors in the dish. Finding the right balance takes some trial and error. If a recipe says simply to season your ingredients, start with a generous pinch of salt and a smaller pinch of pepper. Try to taste your ingredients throughout the cooking process to make sure they are properly seasoned.

SIMMERING VERSUS BOILING

If a recipe says to heat a liquid to a simmer, look for small bubbles that rise to the liquid's surface, causing gentle movement. If a recipe calls for boiling the liquid, look for many large bubbles rising at once, constantly disrupting the liquid's surface.

TOSSING TOGETHER

Tossing refers to mixing ingredients lightly until one is well-coated with the other. For example, potatoes, celery, and onion are tossed with a dressing to make potato salad. This requires more of an upward motion than stirring. Tossing also refers to mixing solid ingredients that remain separate, such as tossing two different types of cheese to create a cheese blend. This kind of tossing is often done with clean hands instead of a spoon or spatula.

SWEATING EGGPLANT

"Sweating" an eggplant refers to drawing out some of the moisture inside of it by sprinkling it with salt and letting it rest. Removing this moisture helps concentrate the eggplant's flavor. Some cooks argue this is not an essential step, so if you are short on time, skip the sweat!

KITCHEN PREP TIPS

> Have all your supplies out and ready before you begin. Gather all your ingredients on a tray or rimmed baking sheet. Then it's easy to slide everything out of the way if you need to make space.
> Wear an apron to protect your clothing. It will also serve as a hand towel.

FOOD PREP TIPS & TRICKS

A successful catered event starts with proper food prep. Here are a few tips and tricks for preparing the recipes in this book.

Herbs should be washed before serving. Swish them around in a large bowl of cold water, then let them float for about 30 seconds before shaking them out. This lets any dirt or sand on the herbs sink down to the bottom of the bowl. This same method can be used to wash lettuce and other leafy greens.

To avoid soggy herbs, thoroughly dry them after washing. A salad spinner is a great tool for this. If you don't have a spinner, lay the herbs on a towel in a single layer and let them air-dry. This same method can be used to dry leafy greens.

If you cannot find phyllo shells for the appetizer on page 30, use phyllo sheets instead. Spread melted butter over a sheet, then place another sheet on top. Repeat until you have five layers. Cut the layered sheets into squares. Press the squares into a greased muffin pan to form cups.

Fudgy brownies should be moist but not undercooked. Test for doneness by sticking a toothpick into the brownies at the center of the pan. If it comes out with wet batter on it, the brownies need more time in the oven. If it comes out with moist crumbs sticking to it, the brownies are ready!

FOOD SAFETY TIPS

- Make sure your prep surface is clean and dry. Wash your hands with soap and water before and after you handle ingredients.
- Don't eat uncooked eggs or meat. Thoroughly wash your hands and all surfaces after handling raw meat.
- Place any leftover ingredients into containers with lids. Use tape and markers to label each container with the ingredient and the date. Keep the containers somewhere you will easily see them so you don't forget about them.

SPEED & SAFETY

Time management and food safety are top priorities for a catering professional. Below are a few guidelines for any catering service.

Prep as many ingredients as possible before the catered event. Peel and chop produce, prepare sauces, and even precook foods that can then be reheated during meal service. This will expedite your service on the day of the event.

Use separate cutting boards for raw food, cooked food, and fresh produce. This prevents cross-contamination. Separate boards and prep surfaces should also be used to prepare meals for guests with food allergies.

Food service professionals follow a rule known as FIFO. It stands for "First In, First Out." This means using up the ingredients that have been in the refrigerator or pantry longest. You can easily follow this rule by stocking newer products behind the older ones so older ones get used first. Just don't use expired products!

Make sure the blade of your knife is sharp. A dull blade is more dangerous than a sharp one because it requires more force to cut through ingredients.

CREATING IN THE KITCHEN

Recipes are great for learning how to cook. But as you get comfortable following recipes, you might start imagining ways to improve them.

Maybe you want to add a cream cheese swirl to your brownies. Or maybe you decide to use radishes instead of celery in your potato salad recipe.

This book includes four formal recipes meant to help you practice working with different ingredients and techniques. Following each formal recipe is an informal companion. These companion recipes are less structured and provide fewer details. This leaves room for you, the cook, to follow your own tastes and preferences. If an informal recipe doesn't suit your taste, check out the accompanying "Experiment!" sidebar for additional ideas. With some thought and creativity, you can make any recipe your own way.

CONVERSION CHART

Standard	Metric
¼ teaspoon	1.25 mL
½ teaspoon	2.5 mL
1 teaspoon	5 mL
1 tablespoon	15 mL
¼ cup	60 mL
⅓ cup	80 mL
½ cup	125 mL
⅔ cup	160 mL
¾ cup	175 mL
1 cup	240 mL
165°F	74°C
325°F	160°C
350°F	180°C
375°F	190°C
400°F	200°C

RULES TO REMEMBER

As you start putting your own twist on recipes, keep these guiding principles in mind.

Master the basics first. Start out following recipes exactly as they are written. You'll better understand how ingredients combine and behave, and this knowledge will inform your decisions as you go off-book.

Every cook has their own methods. You might see another cook bake their chicken Parmesan instead of frying it. Or, another cook may cube their potatoes before boiling them instead of after. This doesn't mean you have to change your ingredients or techniques. If you can, ask a cook why their methods work for them. Test the methods yourself and decide what works best for you!

Experiments don't always go to plan. Don't be crushed if you overbaked your brownies or under-seasoned your spinach. If the results are still edible, don't let them go to waste! Instead, think of how you can make them tastier. If your brownies are dry, top them with frosting or caramel sauce. If your spinach appetizers are bland, top them with grated Parmesan, crispy bacon, or another salty ingredient.

Cooking is often called an art, not a science. A recipe won't be ruined by an extra hit of lemon juice or a missed teaspoon of garlic powder. Cooks are always tweaking and testing their recipes. Enjoy the process and take pride in the results.

MAKE THIS!

APPETIZER

SPINACH & FETA CUPS

Pass around these bite-size appetizers to keep hungry guests happy!

INGREDIENTS

- > 10-ounce (283.5 g) package frozen spinach, thawed
- > ¼ cup mayonnaise
- > ¼ cup ricotta
- > 1 teaspoon lemon juice
- > ½ teaspoon garlic powder
- > ½ teaspoon kosher salt
- > ¼ teaspoon black pepper
- > ½ cup crumbled feta
- > about 25 frozen phyllo shells

SUPPLIES

- > oven
- > paper towels
- > sieve or colander (optional)
- > rubber spatula
- > large mixing bowl
- > measuring cups and spoons
- > whisk
- > baking sheet
- > cooling rack

1

Preheat the oven to 350°F. Use paper towels to squeeze as much moisture from the thawed spinach as possible. You can also place the spinach in a colander or sieve and press on it with a rubber spatula.

2

In the mixing bowl, whisk together the mayonnaise, ricotta cheese, lemon juice, garlic powder, salt, and pepper.

3

Add the spinach and feta to the bowl.

4

Use the rubber spatula to mix everything together.

5

Place the phyllo shells onto a baking sheet. Divide the mixture among the shells.

6

Bake the spinach and feta bites for 10 to 15 minutes or until the cheese is a light golden color. Let them cool slightly before serving.

MAKE IT YOUR WAY

BRIE & JAM
CUPS

When it comes to filling phyllo shells, the ingredient combinations are endless. Try this simple but decadent brie-and-jam combo!

Place a slice of brie cheese into each phyllo shell.

EXPERIMENT!

What other flavor combinations can you play with? Tomato and mozzarella? Mushroom and Swiss? Bacon and cheddar? Think about how you might make taco bites, pizza bites, or even macaroni and cheese bites!

Top the brie with about 1 teaspoon of jam or preserves of your choice. If you'd like, add some sliced almonds or chopped walnuts to each cup.

Bake the bites at 350°F for seven to nine minutes.

MAKE THIS!

MAIN COURSE

CHICKEN PARMESAN

This classic Italian dish of breaded chicken, mozzarella, and marinara is a widely popular catered meal.

INGREDIENTS

- 2 chicken breasts
- kosher salt and black pepper for seasoning
- 1 egg
- ½ tablespoon water
- ¾ teaspoon garlic powder
- ¾ teaspoon onion powder
- ¼ cup plus 2 tablespoons all-purpose flour
- 2 tablespoons cornstarch
- 1 cup panko
- vegetable oil
- 2 cups jarred marinara sauce
- 1½ cups shredded mozzarella
- 1 cup grated Parmesan
- ¼ cup chopped fresh parsley

SUPPLIES

- knife and cutting board
- mixing bowls
- measuring cups and spoons
- whisk
- tray
- cooling rack
- paper towels
- Dutch oven
- stove
- thermometer(s) for oil and chicken
- tongs
- oven
- baking dish

1. Cut each chicken breast in half horizontally, creating four cutlets. Season both sides of each cutlet with salt and pepper.

2. In one bowl, whisk together the egg, water, garlic powder, and onion powder.

3. In another bowl, whisk together the flour and cornstarch. Pour the panko in a third bowl.

4. Take one cutlet and dredge it in the flour mixture.

5. Dip the floured cutlet into the egg mixture until coated. Let excess egg drip back into the bowl.

6. Lay the cutlet in the panko, firmly pressing the cutlet into the breadcrumbs so it is completely coated on both sides. Place the cutlet on a tray.

7 Repeat steps 4 through 6 with the remaining cutlets.

8 Fill the Dutch oven with about 1 inch (2.5 cm) of oil and heat it over medium-high heat until the thermometer reads 350°F.

9 Prep the cooling rack by placing it over a few layers of paper towels, which will absorb dripping grease later.

10 Using tongs, carefully place one cutlet into the hot oil. Cook the chicken for about five minutes, turning it with tongs every couple minutes, until it is golden brown and has an internal temperature of 165°F. Place the cooked cutlet on the cooling rack.

11 Once the oil temperature returns to 350°F, repeat step 10 to cook the remaining cutlets.

12 Turn on the oven's broiler. Place the cutlets in a baking dish and top each with ½ cup marinara sauce.

13 Toss the mozzarella and Parmesan cheeses together in a mixing bowl. Then sprinkle about ½ cup of the cheese blend over each cutlet.

14 Place the baking dish under the broiler for about five minutes or until the cheese is golden and bubbly.

15 Let the cutlets cool slightly, then garnish them with the chopped parsley before serving.

MAKE IT YOUR WAY

EGGPLANT
PARMESAN

Provide a meatless option for vegetarian guests by replacing the chicken with eggplant!

Cut an eggplant into slices about ½ inch (1.3 cm) thick. Salt both sides of each slice and let the eggplant sweat for about 30 minutes. Then use a paper towel to dry the slices.

EXPERIMENT!

Try roasting your eggplant slices in the oven instead of frying them in oil. Whip up your own homemade marinara instead of using jarred sauce. Stack a few layers of the eggplant, sauce, and cheese to create an eggplant lasagna.

Bread the eggplant slices as you would chicken cutlets. Heat 1 inch (2.5 cm) of oil to 350°F and fry the eggplant for one to two minutes on each side.

Spread a layer of marinara sauce over the bottom of a baking dish. Add the fried eggplant slices, more sauce, mozzarella, and Parmesan. Broil until the cheese is golden.

MAKE THIS!

SIDE POTATO SALAD

To accompany a main course, caterers can offer a variety of side salads built on greens, grains, and more. Try this classic salad featuring the much-loved potato.

INGREDIENTS

- 2 pounds (0.9 kg) yellow potatoes
- about 8 cups cold water
- ¼ cup kosher salt, plus more for seasoning
- ⅔ cup mayonnaise
- 1 tablespoon mustard
- 2 tablespoons apple cider vinegar
- 1 teaspoon granulated sugar
- ½ teaspoon garlic salt
- black pepper for seasoning
- ½ cup diced red onion
- ½ cup diced celery
- 1 tablespoon minced chives

SUPPLIES

- large pot with cover
- measuring cups and spoons
- stove
- fork
- mixing bowl
- whisk
- colander
- knife and cutting board
- rubber spatula

Place the potatoes in the large pot. Add enough cold water to cover the potatoes by 1 inch (2.5 cm). Pour in the salt.

Cover the pot and set it over medium-high heat until the water comes to a gentle boil. Then take off the cover and continue to cook the potatoes for about 15 minutes or until they are fork-tender.

While the potatoes cook, whisk together in a mixing bowl the mayonnaise, mustard, apple cider vinegar, sugar, and garlic salt. Season with black pepper.

4

Drain the cooked potatoes. Let them sit for 10 minutes or until they are cool enough to handle. Then cut them into ½-inch (1.3 cm) cubes.

5

Add the cubed potatoes to the dressing and gently toss to coat all potatoes.

6

Add the chopped celery and onion and gently toss to incorporate. Season the salad with salt, pepper, and minced chives before serving.

MAKE IT YOUR WAY

GARLIC MASHED
POTATOES

If you'd prefer a warm and steamy side, whip your cooked potatoes with garlicky cream for some ever-popular mashed potatoes.

Heat ½ cup heavy cream, 2 tablespoons butter, and 2 crushed cloves of garlic in a saucepan until it simmers. Take the pan off the heat, cover it, and set it aside while you boil the potatoes.

EXPERIMENT!

Steep other herbs, such as rosemary or thyme, in the hot cream. Try roasting the garlic cloves in the oven and then whipping them into the potatoes. Experiment with other add-ins, such as sour cream, Greek yogurt, or grated cheese.

Remove the crushed garlic from the cream. Use an electric mixer to whip the warm cream into the cooked potatoes.

Season your mashed potatoes with salt and pepper, and serve with a garnish of minced chives.

MAKE THIS!

DESSERT
BROWNIE BITES

Event guests love mini desserts because they can try one of everything. Brownie bites are a simple sweet treat to cap off a catered meal.

INGREDIENTS

- > vegetable oil or baking spray for greasing
- > 1 stick (8 tablespoons) butter
- > ½ cup semisweet chocolate chips
- > 1 cup granulated sugar
- > 2 eggs
- > 2 teaspoons vanilla extract
- > ½ cup all-purpose flour
- > ½ cup cocoa powder
- > ¼ teaspoon kosher salt
- > powdered sugar for dusting

SUPPLIES

- > oven
- > mini muffin pan
- > microwave
- > large microwave-safe mixing bowl
- > measuring cups and spoons
- > spoon
- > whisk
- > small mixing bowl
- > rubber spatula
- > spoon
- > knife
- > cooling rack
- > baking sheet
- > sieve

1 Preheat the oven to 350°F. Grease the mini muffin pan.

2 Microwave the butter and chocolate chips in the large mixing bowl in 25-second intervals, stirring between each interval, until the mixture is smooth.

Add the eggs and vanilla extract to the mixture and whisk until they are fully incorporated.

Whisk the sugar into the melted chocolate until it is fully incorporated.

In the smaller bowl, whisk together the flour, cocoa powder, and salt.

6

Gradually stir the dry mixture into the wet mixture until fully combined.

7

Spoon the batter into the muffin cups. Bake the brownie bites for about 15 minutes, or until the tops are cracked and dry.

8 Let the brownies cool in the pan on a cooling rack for 10 minutes. Then run a knife around each brownie to help lift it out of the pan. Place the brownie bites on a cooling rack to continue cooling.

9

Once the bites are fully cooled, move them to a baking sheet and use the sieve to dust them with powdered sugar.

MAKE IT YOUR WAY

BROWNIE
POPS

Turn your brownie bites into fun pops with candy melts and sprinkles!

Bake your brownie batter in an 8-by-8-inch (20.3 by 20.3 cm) pan lined with parchment paper for about 30 minutes. Cut the baked brownie into 2-inch (5.1 cm) squares.

EXPERIMENT!

Try crumbling your baked brownies into a bowl and mixing it with frosting before scooping it into balls. Dip your pops into melted chocolate instead of candy melts. Instead of using sprinkles, drizzle a second candy melt color over the first layer.

Shape the brownie squares into balls and insert a lollipop stick into each. Freeze the brownie pops for about two hours.

Microwave candy melts until they are smooth. Dip the brownie pops into the candy melt coating and then decorate them with sprinkles.

PRESENTATION & BEYOND

Your dish is complete, but you're not done yet! It's time to think about how you want to serve, display, or package your creation. Catering professionals and event organizers work together to come up with a service style that best suits the menu and event.

Place appetizers on trays for waitstaff to circulate among guests. Or, display appetizers on serving tables for guests to grab at their leisure.

Main courses can be plated by catering staff and served to seated guests. Caterers can also keep dishes warm on the buffet table using chafing dishes. These are metal pans heated by hot water.

Salads and other side dishes can be plated with the main course, served in chafing dishes, or portioned into individual, easy-to-grab containers.

Desserts are often the most visually fun part of a catered meal. Get creative with their display!

SPECIAL CONSIDERATIONS

Many catered events, such as sporting events and boxed-lunch meetings, require disposable packaging and utensils. For events like these, many customers care about environmental impact more than ever. They favor catering professionals who do everything they can to minimize waste, reduce plastic use, and use plant-based compostable products. Catering professionals must consider these preferences when deciding how they will package and serve their food.

CAREERS IN THE KITCHEN

BECOMING A CATERING PROFESSIONAL

As you gain more knowledge and experience cooking for a crowd, you might decide to turn your hobby into a living. There are many ways to pursue a career in catering!

CULINARY SCHOOL
Culinary and technical schools offer culinary arts programs that last anywhere from a few months to several years. These programs offer instruction in knife skills, food safety, presentation, and more. They also prepare students for work in professional kitchens.

BUSINESS SCHOOL
Business schools offer courses in accounting, management, marketing, and other topics related to running a business. Business programs last two or more years, depending on the degree you are seeking.

ON-THE-JOB TRAINING
Many catering companies hire employees with no formal culinary training. New cooks learn how to prepare the dishes from experienced coworkers.

SELF-TEACHING
Many professional cooks and business owners learned what they know by doing their own research, watching others, making mistakes, and trying again. Many entrepreneurs follow this self-teaching path to start their own businesses.

CATERING PROS AT WORK

Catering professionals work in numerous roles in a variety of establishments. Read about a few of them below. Think about which suit you best and why.

ESTABLISHMENTS

Many catering professionals work at catering companies. These companies may offer a range of catering services or specialize in certain events, such as weddings. Catering professionals can also find work at hotels, restaurants, and grocery stores that have catering departments. Finally, many independent chefs operate their own catering businesses from their personal kitchens or rented commercial kitchens.

ROLES

Any food service operation needs a chef to plan and oversee food prep and meal service. Sous-chefs and other kitchen staff assist in executing these tasks. Meanwhile, servers prepare the dining area and serve food and drinks to event guests. Catering businesses also need catering managers. These professionals help plan the menu, communicate with clients, manage the budget, coordinate schedules, and more.

Working in a catering kitchen can be drastically different from home cooking. As you think about working in catering, consider some of the tools, rules, and schedules of the industry.

TOOLS

Most commercial kitchens require large refrigerators, ovens, ranges, and other industrial equipment to store and prepare large volumes of food. Caterers require additional equipment for transporting and serving the food. Catering carts are wheeled carts with multiple shelves meant to transport ingredients and prepared food from the kitchen to the event site. Portable buffet stations and beverage carts are often placed in the dining area so guests can serve themselves.

themselves and others from common kitchen hazards, such as hot pans and wet floors.

RULES

Catering professionals must uphold cleanliness and food safety standards. These standards range from wearing a uniform and keeping hair pulled back to properly storing ingredients and thoroughly cleaning equipment after use. Kitchen staff must also follow rules to protect

SCHEDULES

Many catering professionals offer their services for any meal of the day, any day of the week. But prep for a catered event often begins days in advance. Catering managers and chefs follow detailed prep schedules so the day of the event runs as smoothly as possible. Kitchen staff arrive hours before the event to prep for service and stay after service to clean up.

Do What You Love!

Being a catering professional requires long shifts, hard physical work, and attention to rules and standards. These requirements can be difficult for home cooks to adjust to. But many professionals find the rewards of their work outweigh the difficulties. These rewards include being creative, getting exercise, and learning new skills.

Maybe your goal is to be a chef for a catering company. Maybe you have your sights set on starting your own catering business. Or perhaps you are happy to keep cooking as a hobby, but not as a career. As long as you do what you love, you'll love what you do.

GLOSSARY

appliance—a household or office device operated by gas or electric power. Common kitchen appliances include stoves, refrigerators, and dishwashers.

aromatic—a strong-smelling vegetable, herb, or spice that adds flavor to a dish.

compostable—able to be broken down into compost, which is a mixture of decayed organics that can be used in growing plants.

COVID-19—a serious illness that first appeared in late 2019.

culinary—having to do with the kitchen or cooking.

edible—safe to eat.

embellish—to make something more attractive by adding details.

enhance—to increase or make better.

entrepreneur—one who organizes, manages, and accepts the risks of a business or an enterprise.

establishment—a place or organization where people do business.

expedite—to speed up.

incorporate—to include or work into.

industrial—of or having to do with factories and making things in large quantities.

leavener—a substance that creates air in a dough or batter to make it rise.

Middle Ages—a period in European history from about 500 CE to about 1500 CE.

pandemic—the worldwide spread of a disease.

plant-based—consisting of fruits, vegetables, grains, and other foods derived from plants while excluding animal products, such as meat or dairy.

portable—able to be carried easily.

soggy—heavy and overly moist.

sous-chef—the second-in-command chef in a restaurant kitchen, who works immediately under the head chef.

technique—a method or style in which something is done.

utensil—a tool, such as a spoon, used for a particular purpose.

waitstaff—employees who serve food and drinks to customers or guests at a restaurant or event.

World War II—from 1939 to 1945, fought in Europe, Asia, and Africa. Great Britain, France, the United States, the Soviet Union, and their allies were on one side. Germany, Italy, Japan, and their allies were on the other side.

ONLINE RESOURCES

To learn more about careers in catering, please visit **abdobooklinks.com** or scan this QR code. These links are routinely monitored and updated to provide the most current information available.

INDEX

appetizers, 8, 23, 29, 31, 54

baking, 12-13, 15-17, 19-20, 29, 31, 33, 37, 39, 49, 51-52
  dishes, 37, 39, 41
  sheets, 15, 22, 31, 33, 49, 51
batter, 12, 16, 19, 23, 51-52
black pepper, 13, 20, 31-32, 37-38, 43-45, 47
boil, 20, 29, 44, 46
Britain, 7
broilers, 15, 39, 41
brownies, 11, 16, 20, 23, 27, 29, 49, 51-53
buffets, 7-8, 54, 59
business, 7, 57-58, 61

candy melts, 11, 52-53
catering
  professional, 5, 25, 54-55, 57-59, 61
  rules, 25, 29, 59, 61
  schedules, 58-59
  staff, 7, 54, 58-59
  tools, 5, 8, 59
cheese, 11, 19, 21, 27, 31-34, 37, 39-41, 46
chicken, 11, 15, 18, 29, 37-41
China, 7
chocolate, 11, 13, 17, 19, 49-50, 52
cleanliness, 21, 24, 59
cocoa powder, 11, 49-51
colanders, 15, 31-32, 43
condiments, 12, 31-32, 43-45
cooling racks, 15, 31, 33, 37, 39, 49, 51
cornstarch, 12, 37-38
COVID-19 pandemic, 8

dairy, 12, 16, 46-47
desserts, 8, 11, 16, 19, 49, 55
dredging, 18, 38
Dutch ovens, 15, 37, 39

eggplant, 18, 21, 40-41
eggs, 12, 17-18, 24, 37-38, 49-50
Egypt, 7
electric mixers, 16, 47

FIFO rule, 25
flour, 12, 17-19, 37-38, 49-50
fork-tender, 19, 44

garnishing, 12, 19, 39, 47
greasing the pan, 13, 19, 23, 50
Greeks, 7
guests, 7-8, 25, 31, 40, 49, 54, 58-59

herbs, 12-13, 19, 23, 37, 39, 43, 45, 46
hotels, 7, 58

Italy, 37

kitchens, 57-59
  tools, 15-17, 59
knives, 18-19, 25, 37-41, 43, 45, 49, 51-52, 57

lollipop sticks, 16, 53

marinara sauce, 13, 37, 39-41
meals, 7-8, 25, 37, 49, 55, 58-59
menus, 5, 7-8, 54, 58
Middle Ages, 7
mixing ingredients, 12-13, 16-17, 19, 21, 32-33, 38-39, 44, 47, 50-52
muffin pans, 16, 23, 49-51

oil, 12-13, 17-19, 37, 39-41, 49-50

panko, 13, 37-38, 41
parchment paper, 16, 52
phyllo, 13, 23, 31, 33-34
potatoes, 15-16, 19, 21, 27, 29, 43-47

preheating oven, 20, 32, 50
presentation, 5, 8, 54, 57

recipes
  brie and jam cups, 34-35
  brownie bites, 49-51
  brownie pops, 52-53
  chicken Parmesan, 37-39
  eggplant Parmesan, 40-41
  garlic mashed potatoes, 46-47
  potato salad, 43-45
  spinach and feta cups, 31-33
restaurants, 7, 58
Romans, 7

safety, 5, 8, 24-25, 57, 59
salt, 11, 13, 20-21, 29, 31-32, 37-38, 40, 43-45, 47, 49-50
saucepans, 16, 46
seasoning, 20, 37-38, 43-45, 47
service, 5, 7-8, 25, 54, 58-59
sieves, 17, 31-32, 49, 51
simmer, 20, 46
spices, 13, 29, 31-32
sugar, 11, 17, 19, 43-44, 49-51

thermometers, 17, 37, 39
tongs, 17, 37, 39
training, 5, 57

United States, 7

vanilla extract, 13, 49-50
vegetables, 13, 18, 21, 23, 25, 31-34, 43, 45

weddings, 7, 58
whisks, 17, 19, 31-32, 37-38, 43-44, 49-50
World War II, 7

64